TRANSFORMATIVE TALKS AND WORDS OF INSPIRATION

HOW AFFIRMATIONS TRANSFORM LIVES

DR. MINAKSHI BANSAL

DEDICATION

This book is dedicated to all those who dare to dream of a better life and are brave enough to make those dreams a reality. To those who face their daily challenges with courage and grace, and who seek every day to be the best versions of themselves. Your resilience inspires me and this journey of writing would not have been the same without the stories and experiences shared by many of you.

To my family, who has supported me unconditionally, your love and encouragement have been my anchor and guide. You have been the first to hear my dreams and the last to remind me of them when the road got tough. This book is a testament to your unwavering belief in me.

And finally, to all who find this book in their hands, may these pages serve as a reminder that your words have power, your thoughts have strength, and your intentions can manifest reality. May you find solace, strength, and joy in your affirmations as you journey towards your best self.

ᐅᐅᐅ

Contents

Contents

Prayer

This mantra is a prayer for universal well-being, invoking the blessings of various deities for protection, health, and happiness. It emphasizes the importance of experiencing the auspicious through all senses and living a life aligned with divine purpose. The repetition of "Shantih" at the end signifies a deep desire for peace in the individual, the environment, and the universe at large. This mantra is often recited as a prayer for peace, prosperity, and the physical and spiritual well-being of all beings.

🍃🍃🍃

About The Author

Dr. Minakshi Bansal, born in the bustling metropolis of Delhi, India, has led a life steeped in artistry, scholarly pursuit, and an unwavering commitment to societal betterment. Following her marriage, she relocated to Ahmedabad, Gujarat, where she has since blossomed into a multifaceted beacon of inspiration for many. Dr. Minakshi is not only recognized as a gifted artist in the realm of Fine Arts but also as an esteemed author, a devoted social worker and a dedicated research scholar in Psychology. Her journey, marked by a profound dedication to elevating those around her, especially the downtrodden and underprivileged children of society, is a testament to her deep-seated belief in the transformative power of engagement and empathy.

From her earliest days, Minakshi was distinguished by an insatiable appetite for reading. Her literary universe was inhabited by characters and narratives that spanned ethical tales, motivational and inspirational stories, and the mythic parables imbued with life lessons. This voracious reading habit was not merely for personal edification but was driven by a desire to distill and disseminate the essence of these narratives to foster the development of students and peers alike. She was particularly captivated by the lives and teachings of historical figures and spiritual leaders such as Adi Shankaracharya, Swami Vivekananda, Dr. APJ Abdul Kalam, Mahamana Pandit Madan Mohan Malviya, Mahatma Gandhi, Sardar Vallabhai Patel, and Vinoba Bhave, among others. Their philosophies and life stories fueled her ambition to embody their ideals of resilience, selflessness, and relentless pursuit of knowledge.

Dr. Minakshi's academic and practical engagement with psychology has been equally noteworthy. As a research scholar, her focus has been on exploring the intricate tapestry of the human psyche, aiming to unlock the potential for psychological well-being and societal harmony. Her scholarly work is complemented by her active involvement in social work, where she employs her academic insights to make tangible differences in the lives of the underprivileged. Her endeavours in social work are characterized by an innovative approach that combines traditional wisdom with contemporary psychological practices to address the multifaceted challenges faced by these communities.

Her artistic talents, another facet of her diverse capabilities, are not merely a personal passion but also serve as a medium through which she communicates and connects with others. Her art, rich in symbolism and emotional depth, reflects her philosophical inquiries and social concerns, offering viewers a glimpse into the breadth of her intellect and the depth of her compassion.

In addition to her contributions to the arts and social sciences, Dr. Minakshi has embraced the healing arts of Pranic Healing, mastering the techniques developed by Master Choa Kok Sui. This practice, which focuses on the manipulation of Prana or life energy to heal the body and aura, has been both a personal journey of discovery and a means through which she extends her healing touch to others. Her proficiency in Pranic Healing is complemented by her advocacy and teaching of various forms of meditation aimed at rejuvenation, personal betterment, and the cultivation of harmony within individuals and communities alike.

Dr. Minakshi's life is a narrative of relentless pursuit, not just of personal achievement but of the upliftment and empowerment of society at large. Her diverse interests and talents—spanning the arts, literature, psychology, and the healing practices—converge on a singular path of service. She embodies the spirit of the luminaries who inspired her, channelling their legacy through her actions and teachings. Through her books, art, and social initiatives, she continues to inspire a new generation to embark on their own journeys of self-discovery, resilience, and altruism.

Her commitment to social betterment, particularly her focus on uplifting underprivileged children, reflects a deep understanding of the transformative potential of education and personal development. By integrating her knowledge of psychology, her artistic sensibilities, and her healing practices, Dr. Bansal has developed a holistic approach to social work that addresses both the immediate needs and the long-term well-being of the communities she serves.

As an author, Dr. Minakshi's writings offer a blend of inspirational insights, practical wisdom, and reflective contemplations drawn from her extensive reading and life experiences. Her books serve as a guide for those seeking to navigate the complexities of life with grace, resilience, and purpose. Through her narratives, she extends an invitation to her readers to explore the depths of their own potential and to contribute meaningfully to the collective well-being of society.

In Dr. Minakshi Bansal, we find a remarkable synthesis of the artist, the scholar, the healer, and the social activist. Her life's work stands as a beacon of hope and a source of inspiration for individuals seeking to make a difference in the world. Her story is a compelling reminder of the power of individual action, rooted in compassion and driven by a profound commitment to the betterment of humanity. Dr. Minakshi's legacy is not just in the tangible outcomes of her efforts but in the enduring spirit of inquiry, empathy, and service that she embodies.

ϷϷϷ

Preface

In the pages of this book, I have endeavoured to explore the profound impact of affirmations on our lives. The power of words to shape thoughts, alter feelings, and, ultimately, transform lives is a subject that has long fascinated me both as a writer and as a person committed to personal and communal growth. This fascination stems from my own journey, one punctuated by moments of self-doubt and triumph, despair and joy—experiences common to us all. What I have found, and what I hope to convey through this book, is that the deliberate use of affirmations can guide us through the tumultuous seas of these experiences, providing a beacon of stability and strength.

Affirmations are, at their core, tools of intent—simple yet powerful declarations that we make to the universe and to ourselves. They are reflections of our deepest values, hopes, and beliefs. When articulated consistently, these affirmations have the capacity to mold our reality, steering us toward positive outcomes. This book delves into how such a simple practice can yield extensive changes in various aspects of life, from personal health and happiness to parenting and professional success.

The idea that the mind can exert a significant influence over one's reality is not new. Philosophers, spiritual leaders, and even scientists have long acknowledged the interplay between thought and experience. However, in our daily grind, it is all too easy to forget that our internal dialogue can shape our external circumstances. Herein lies the true value of affirmations—they help us rewrite that internal dialogue, replacing self-defeating thoughts with narratives of empowerment and hope.

Each chapter of this book has been crafted to not only provide insights into different aspects of life that can be enhanced by affirmations but also to offer practical guidelines on how to create and use affirmations effectively. Whether it is fostering self-esteem, overcoming fear, or nurturing relationships, affirmations can play a pivotal role in cultivating a life of fulfillment and joy. Moreover, by sharing these affirmations within a community, we can extend their benefits, strengthening bonds and fostering an environment of support and encouragement.

Drawing upon a diverse range of sources, from psychological studies to anecdotal evidence, this book presents a comprehensive look at the mechanisms through which affirmations work. It explores the scientific underpinnings of how positive self-talk strengthens neural pathways, the psychological benefits of fostering a positive mindset, and the spiritual uplift that many derive from this practice.

What is particularly enchanting about affirmations is their universality and simplicity. They require no special tools or training—just a moment of reflection, a dash of belief, and a commitment to repeated practice. This accessibility makes affirmations a powerful tool for anyone, irrespective of age, background, or circumstance. It is my hope that by sharing both my personal experiences and the extensive research I've encountered, this book will serve as both a guide and an inspiration for readers looking to enhance their lives through the power of affirmations.

In writing this book, I have been reminded of the transformative power of words each day. It has been a journey of self-discovery and reaffirmation, and my aim is for each reader to experience a similar journey. As you turn these pages and explore the various facets of using affirmations, I invite you to open your heart and mind to the possibilities they might bring. Try them, tweak them, and make them your own. With each affirmation, you are not merely hoping for a better future; you are actively constructing it with the most powerful tool at your disposal—your own words.

Thus, let this book be a companion on your journey to a more fulfilled and empowered existence. The affirmations provided here are starting points—seeds that, when nurtured with belief and consistency, can grow into the very pillars of your life's joy and success. I encourage you to embrace this simple yet profound practice, to let it transform your inner dialogue, and to watch as it transforms your life in turn.

Dr. Minakshi Bansal
Social Activist
Ahmedabad, Gujarat, Bharat

ONE

INTRODUCTION TO AFFIRMATIONS

Affirmations are simple, positive statements that, when repeated frequently, have the power to encourage and sustain an internal change in our thinking pattern and attitude towards life. These statements are designed to alter the subconscious mind's narrative, often cluttered with doubts and negativity, and replace it with confidence and optimism. This fundamental shift can significantly influence our perception of the world, enabling us to maintain a more positive outlook on our lives and circumstances.

The effectiveness of affirmations lies in their simplicity and the personal connection they foster. An affirmation like "I am capable and strong" can serve as a powerful psychological boost. When faced with challenges, repeating such phrases can remind us of our strengths, thereby fostering a sense of competence and resilience. This method harnesses the power of positive thinking to combat the often automatic tendency of the mind to focus on fears and limitations.

The Foundation of Affirmations

Affirmations find their roots in various psychological theories, including cognitive behavioral therapy (CBT) and neuro-linguistic programming (NLP), which emphasize the role of self-talk in shaping our mental and emotional well-being. By consciously choosing our thoughts through targeted affirmations, we can create an environment in our minds that promotes well-being and effectiveness. This practice is not just about fostering positive thinking but about setting a foundation for real changes in how we feel and act.

Every thought we have is a catalyst for neural changes. Neuroscientific research suggests that positive affirmations can stimulate the brain areas that make us less susceptible to criticism and more adaptable to challenges, enhancing our ability to view the world positively. Regular practice of affirmations reinforces this effect, embedding these positive beliefs into our neural pathways.

Practical Application of Affirmations in Daily Life

Integrating affirmations into daily life can begin with identifying areas where we seek improvement or support. For instance, someone struggling with self-esteem may choose affirmations that reinforce their worth and capabilities. It's crucial that these affirmations are stated in the present tense, feel believable, and focus on positive attributes. For example, instead of saying "I will be successful," a more immediate and believable statement would be "I am becoming more successful every day."

The key to making affirmations work is consistency. Repeating them daily, ideally at the same time each day, helps in engraving these positive assertions into the subconscious. Morning can be an ideal time for this practice, as it sets a positive tone for the day. However, reaffirming these thoughts during challenging moments can also provide immediate relief and a shift in perspective.

Another effective way to amplify the impact of affirmations is through visualization. Imagining oneself successfully handling a situation or achieving a goal adds a layer of effectiveness to the affirmation. This visualization reinforces the affirmation, making it more tangible and believable.

Integration with Mindfulness and Meditation

For those who practice mindfulness or meditation, affirmations can be a valuable addition to their routine. During meditation, the mind is receptive and calm, making it an ideal time to introduce positive affirmations. This combination not only deepens the meditative practice but also embeds the affirmations more deeply into our thought processes.

Challenges and Considerations

While the benefits of affirmations are significant, they are not a magical cure-all. They work best when combined with real efforts towards personal growth and behavior change. For affirmations to truly be effective, they must be part of a broader approach to self-improvement that includes setting realistic goals and taking concrete steps towards achieving them.

Furthermore, the effectiveness of affirmations can vary from person to person. Skepticism can dampen their impact, as can a lack of alignment between one's values and the affirmations they choose. Therefore, it's essential for individuals to select affirmations that genuinely resonate with their personal aspirations and values.

Affirmations are a powerful tool for transforming our inner dialogue and fostering a positive mindset. They enable us to overcome self-doubt and negativity, offering a simple yet effective method for enhancing our mental landscape. By choosing affirmations that align with our true desires and repeating them regularly, we set the stage for meaningful changes in our thoughts, feelings, and behaviors, ultimately leading to a more fulfilled and optimistic life.

ᚻᚻᚻ

"Affirmations are the architects of our reality;
through them, we construct the framework of our
lives. They allow us to build upon our strengths and
reshape our weaknesses. Every repeated word is a
brick laid in the foundation of our destiny."

ᗡᗡᗡ

TWO
THE SCIENCE BEHIND AFFIRMATIONS

Affirmations, though simple in form, are deeply rooted in both psychological and neurological sciences. They are short, declarative sentences aimed at consciously influencing one's thoughts, which in turn impacts the emotional and physical health. Understanding the dual impact of affirmations—both psychological and neurological—can provide a comprehensive insight into their power and effectiveness in transforming lives.

Psychological Impact of Affirmations

From a psychological standpoint, affirmations can alter the way we perceive ourselves and our capabilities, significantly affecting our overall sense of well-being. According to the theory of cognitive dissonance, when there is a discrepancy between our beliefs and our actions, it creates an inner tension. Affirmations help in aligning our beliefs with our actions, thereby reducing tension and fostering a positive self-concept.

The practice of using affirmations also relates closely to self-affirmation theory, which suggests that actively and positively affirming one's values can protect against the detrimental effects of stress and threats to our self-integrity. This theory posits that affirmations can enhance our resilience by reminding us of important personal values, thus maintaining a positive self-view. When individuals affirm their personal values, they are less likely to react defensively when threatened, which enhances their ability to perceive otherwise threatening information as more relevant and valuable.

Neurological Foundations

Neurologically, affirmations influence the brain's functioning by stimulating the neural pathways associated with self-related processing and reward signals. The brain does not distinguish between reality and vivid imagination; therefore, when affirmations are practiced regularly, they can alter the brain's neural pathways. MRI evidence suggests that certain neural pathways increase in efficiency through the practice of self-affirmation tasks. Particularly, areas of the brain such as the ventromedial prefrontal cortex (VMPFC), which plays a role in positive valuation and self-related information processing, become more active.

This enhanced activity in the VMPFC can lead to an increased sense of self-worth and self-efficacy. By repeatedly focusing on positive outcomes and behaviors, affirmations can reinforce the brain's natural tendency to adapt—known as neuroplasticity—thus creating a more positive, hopeful framework for viewing the world.

Reinforcement through Repetition

The repeated use of affirmations leverages the "Hebbian theory" in neuroscience, which is often summarized as "neurons that fire together, wire together." This principle underlies the idea that repeated activation of certain brain circuits strengthens the associated cognitive habits. When affirmations are repeated, they reinforce the pathway between the belief (cognitive aspect) and the emotional response. Over time, this repeated activation not only makes these thoughts more accessible but also makes them more likely to influence behavior and perception.

Integration with Cognitive Behavioral Therapy (CBT)

Affirmations can be an integral part of Cognitive Behavioral Therapy (CBT), which is a well-established psychological treatment that aims to change patterns of thinking or behavior that are behind people's difficulties, and so change the way they feel. Affirmations in CBT are used as a tool to counter negative thoughts and to reinforce the understanding of one's self-efficacy and coping capabilities. By routinely practicing positive affirmations, clients learn to override the negative patterns of thinking with more adaptive, positive thoughts, which leads to more constructive behaviors.

Practical Application and Effectiveness

The effectiveness of affirmations can be enhanced by incorporating them into daily routines. For instance, starting the day by affirming personal strengths or goals can set a positive tone for the day. It's important that affirmations are personalized and resonate emotionally with the individual, as the emotional connection can amplify the impact on the brain.

Despite their simplicity, the depth of change that affirmations can instigate both psychologically and neurologically is profound. They offer an accessible tool to foster resilience, positivity, and a proactive attitude towards life. Through regular practice, affirmations can not only reshape our internal dialogue but also enhance our overall mental health, providing a solid foundation for personal growth and self-actualization.

In wrapping up, the power of affirmations lies in their ability to transform our psychological and neurological pathways, fostering a mindset that can overcome challenges and seize opportunities. This transformative potential underscores the importance of their thoughtful application in daily life, providing a simple yet effective tool for personal development and emotional health.

ᐅᐅᐅ

"The power of affirmations lies in their simplicity and the personal connection they create. When we speak positive truths into our existence, we light a fire of change that burns away old, limiting beliefs. This transformative power is available to anyone willing to speak it into being."

ppp

THREE

CRAFTING EFFECTIVE AFFIRMATIONS

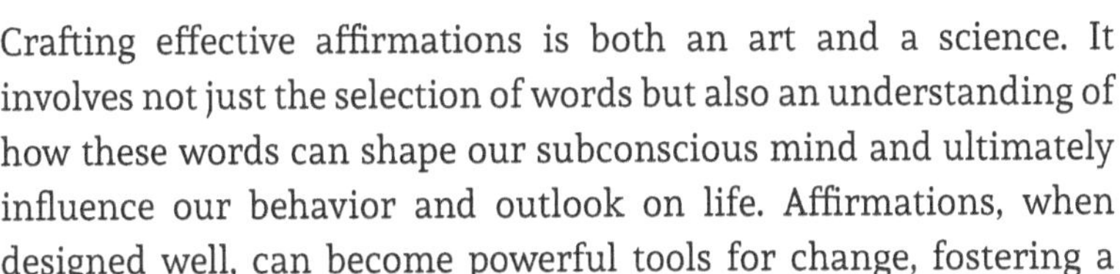

Crafting effective affirmations is both an art and a science. It involves not just the selection of words but also an understanding of how these words can shape our subconscious mind and ultimately influence our behavior and outlook on life. Affirmations, when designed well, can become powerful tools for change, fostering a mindset that enhances resilience, motivation, and overall well-being.

Understanding the Components of Effective Affirmations

The first step in crafting an effective affirmation is understanding its core components. An effective affirmation is clear, positive, present tense, and personal. It should be formulated in a way that is easy to remember and emotionally resonant. The simplicity of the language used is crucial as it helps the mind to easily integrate the affirmation into daily thought processes.

Clarity and Specificity: The affirmation should be straightforward and express exactly what you want to achieve. Ambiguity dilutes the power of the affirmation. For instance, instead of saying "I want to be happy," a more specific affirmation would be "I am enjoying the richness of each day with gratitude."

Present Tense: Affirmations are most effective when they are stated in the present tense. This helps create the belief that the change is currently happening, which can make the affirmation feel more realistic and achievable. For example, "I am confident and competent in my work," as opposed to "I will be confident."

Positivity: It is vital to frame affirmations positively because the subconscious mind often does not process negations directly. Instead of stating what you do not want or wish to avoid, affirmations should focus on what you want to manifest. So, "I am free from fear" should be "I am embracing courage and peace."

Personalization: Affirmations should be personally meaningful. They need to resonate with your personal aspirations and challenges. This connection makes them more powerful and more likely to result in a positive change.

Techniques for Writing Powerful Affirmations

Reflection and Self-Assessment: Begin by identifying areas of your life you wish to improve or feelings you want to cultivate. Reflect on your values, goals, and the challenges that hinder your progress. This reflection will provide a basis for affirmations that are aligned with your true self.

Use Emotionally Charged Words: Words have power, especially those that evoke strong emotional responses. Affirmations that include emotionally charged words are more likely to be impactful. For example, "I am thrilled with my progress and success" is more potent than "I am happy with my progress."

Keep it Short and Memorable: The effectiveness of an affirmation partly relies on its ease of recall. Long, complicated affirmations are less likely to be remembered and therefore less likely to be effective. Keeping them short and simple makes them more practical for daily repetition.

Visualization: While crafting an affirmation, visualize the outcome. Imagining the realization of your affirmation enhances its clarity and impact. If your affirmation is about confidence, picture yourself speaking confidently in a meeting or at a public event.

Consistency in Practice: For affirmations to embed themselves into your subconscious and start manifesting changes, they need to be repeated consistently. Incorporate them into your daily routine, such as saying them every morning, writing them in a journal, or repeating them before bed.

Integration into Everyday Life

Once you have crafted your affirmations, integrating them into your daily life is essential. You can use various methods such as post-it notes in visible places, reminders on your phone, or even affirmation apps that help you track your practice. Regular reflection on the affirmations and their relevance can also help keep them fresh and impactful.

Another powerful way to enhance the impact of your affirmations is to share them with a supportive community or with friends who can provide encouragement. This not only reinforces the affirmation but also creates a network of accountability.

Adaptability and Growth

As you evolve and your circumstances change, so too should your affirmations. Regularly updating your affirmations to reflect your current needs and aspirations keeps them relevant and aligned with your personal growth. This adaptability ensures that the affirmations continue to serve their purpose effectively.

Crafting effective affirmations is a proactive step towards manifesting your desired state of mind and circumstances. By setting clear, positive, and personally meaningful affirmations and integrating them into your daily routine, you can harness their power to significantly alter your thought patterns, emotions, and life outcomes. The simple yet profound practice of affirmations holds the potential to transform challenges into opportunities and dreams into reality, guiding you towards a more fulfilled and purposeful life.

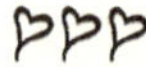

"Integrating affirmations into your daily life is like planting seeds in a garden; with regular care and attention, these seeds grow into the fruits of positivity and success. Each affirmation is a commitment to nourish the soul and cultivate a life of abundance. Over time, what once seemed barren can flourish beyond imagination."

ᚦᚦᚦ

FOUR

MORNING AFFIRMATIONS TO START YOUR DAY

Starting the day with a series of positive affirmations can set the tone for a more optimistic and proactive day. Morning affirmations are powerful tools that energize the spirit, focus the mind, and prepare the individual for the day's challenges and opportunities. By affirming one's value, capabilities, and goals at the beginning of the day, individuals can enhance their resilience against negativity and stress.

The Power of Morning Affirmations

Morning affirmations serve as a psychological primer, setting a mental agenda that emphasizes positivity and self-efficacy. This practice is rooted in the principles of positive psychology, which highlights the importance of nurturing a positive mindset to enhance overall well-being. By starting the day with affirmations, you embed these positive thoughts into your subconscious, helping to shift your usual patterns of thinking towards more uplifting and empowering themes.

Creating a Morning Affirmation Routine

To make the most of morning affirmations, it is beneficial to integrate them into a consistent morning routine. This could be during a morning meditation, while exercising, or even while having breakfast. The key is to choose a time when you can have a few undisturbed minutes to truly focus on and internalize these affirmations.

Quiet and Focused Environment: Choose a place where you feel comfortable and free from distractions. This could be a specific chair, your bed, or a spot in your garden.

Consistency is Key: Make affirming your positive thoughts a daily habit. Consistency helps to reinforce these thoughts and embed them deeply into your psyche.

Visualization: As you recite each affirmation, try to visualize the outcome. For example, if your affirmation is about being productive, imagine yourself handling tasks efficiently throughout the day.

Examples of Morning Affirmations

Here are several examples of morning affirmations that can boost positivity and motivation from the start of the day:

"I am filled with gratitude and joy for another day."

"I possess the qualities needed to be extremely successful."

"My body is healthy; my mind is brilliant; my soul is tranquil."

"I believe I can do anything and everything."

"Today, I am overflowing with energy and joy."

"I am a powerhouse; I am indestructible."

"Today, I will change the world."

"I am the architect of my life; I build its foundation and choose its contents."

"Today, I am brimming with energy and overflowing with joy."

"My thoughts are filled with positivity and my life is plentiful with prosperity."

Each of these affirmations helps to reinforce a positive self-image and a confident outlook on the day ahead. They encourage a shift from passive acceptance of life to an active role in shaping one's destiny.

Tailoring Affirmations to Personal Goals

While general affirmations can be broadly uplifting, customizing affirmations to align with specific personal goals or challenges can enhance their impact. If you have a presentation, an affirmation like "I communicate clearly and confidently" can boost self-assurance. For someone focusing on health goals, "I respect my body and nourish it with what it needs" can reinforce healthy choices.

The Role of Affirmations in Cultivating Mindfulness

Morning affirmations also play a crucial role in cultivating mindfulness. By focusing on these positive statements, you bring your attention to the present moment, grounding yourself in the "now." This practice not only reduces stress but also enhances your awareness of your own mental and emotional state throughout the day.

Challenges and Overcoming Skepticism

It's natural for some individuals to feel skeptical about the efficacy of affirmations. The key to overcoming this skepticism is to understand the psychological and neurological backing of repetitive positive speech. Moreover, personalization of affirmations can significantly increase their relevancy and impact, making the practice feel more genuine and effective.

Incorporating Affirmations into Daily Life

To truly harness the power of morning affirmations, consider integrating them with other positive morning routines, such as journaling, yoga, or a healthy breakfast. This holistic approach to starting the day can amplify the benefits of each individual practice, creating a compound effect of positivity and health.

Morning affirmations are more than just positive statements; they are a catalyst for mental transformation and a proactive approach to daily living. They equip you to handle whatever the day may bring with optimism, resilience, and energy. By establishing a routine of reciting powerful, personalized affirmations each morning, you pave the way for a day led by positivity and a life driven by purpose.

꧁꧁꧁

"Community and affirmations together weave a
tapestry of support and shared growth. When we
echo each other's positive statements, we magnify
their power, creating a resonance that strengthens
not just individuals but the entire group. This
collective energy is a force that can move
mountains."

ϷϷϷ

FIVE

AFFIRMATIONS FOR SELF-ESTEEM

Affirmations for self-esteem are designed to cultivate a sense of intrinsic worth and confidence, providing a foundation from which individuals can live more fully and engage with the world more assertively. When practiced consistently, these affirmations can fundamentally transform one's self-image, reinforcing a positive identity and nurturing an environment where self-respect and confidence flourish.

Understanding Self-Esteem and Its Importance

Self-esteem refers to the overall opinion we have of ourselves—how much we appreciate and like ourselves. It affects every aspect of our lives, from how we operate in our careers, our relationships, to how likely we are to pursue our ambitions. A healthy level of self-esteem allows individuals to face life with more resilience and optimism, helping mitigate the effects of stress and setbacks.

The Impact of Affirmations on Self-Esteem

Affirmations can play a pivotal role in shaping and enhancing one's self-esteem. By affirming one's worth and capabilities, individuals can begin to rewrite the narratives of self-doubt that often reside in the subconscious mind. These positive statements are powerful tools for change, encouraging shifts in thinking that foster a more positive self-view.

Crafting Effective Self-Esteem Affirmations

To craft affirmations that effectively boost self-esteem, it is crucial to focus on statements that reinforce self-acceptance and personal strength. These affirmations should be deeply personal, positively framed, and present-tense to be impactful.

Positive Framing: Affirmations should always be framed positively to encourage a shift towards positive thinking. Instead of focusing on negating negative self-beliefs, affirmations should celebrate positive attributes and strengths. For example, instead of saying, "I am not worthless," say, "I am valuable and unique."

Present Tense: It is also vital that affirmations are framed in the present tense. Saying "I am" rather than "I will be" helps you to believe that the change is currently happening, not something that is delayed to the future.

Personalization: The more personalized an affirmation is, the more effective it will be. Reflect on what aspects of self-esteem you specifically need reinforcement in and tailor your affirmations to address these areas.

Examples of Self-Esteem Affirmations

Here are several powerful affirmations designed to boost self-esteem:

"I am worthy of respect and love."

"I am a unique individual with much to offer."

"I accept myself unconditionally."

"I am proud of my achievements and celebrate my progress."

"I deserve happiness and peace of mind."

"I am confident in my ability to solve problems."

"I am growing and becoming a better version of myself each day."

"I am strong, resilient, and equipped to handle life's challenges."

"I am competent, smart, and able."

"I am valuable and make significant contributions to the world around me."

Integrating Affirmations into Daily Life

To truly benefit from self-esteem affirmations, integrate them into your daily routine. This could be through morning meditation sessions, repeated recitation during daily commutes, or reflection in the evening. It's also helpful to post these affirmations in places where they are regularly seen—on a bathroom mirror, on the dashboard of your car, or as a background on your phone or computer.

Reinforcement Through Repetition

The key to making these affirmations work is repetition. The frequent repetition of positive affirmations helps to make them a part of your subconscious narrative. Over time, these positive assertions become ingrained in your self-perception, gradually replacing negative thoughts and beliefs with positive ones.

Measuring Changes and Adapting Affirmations

As you regularly use affirmations to enhance your self-esteem, it's important to periodically assess their effectiveness and adapt them to your evolving needs. Notice any changes in your feelings of self-worth or confidence in various situations. You may find that some affirmations resonate more deeply or become more relevant as your experiences and self-perception evolve.

Affirmations for self-esteem are a simple yet powerful tool to foster a positive and resilient self-image. They help combat the internal critic and replace it with a supportive voice, enhancing one's sense of self-worth and confidence. With consistent practice, these affirmations can transform your psychological landscape, paving the way for a life characterized by greater fulfillment, confidence, and assertiveness.

ϷϷϷ

"Every affirmation is a step toward overcoming the mountains of doubt and fear that often block our path. With each positive declaration, we equip ourselves with the tools needed to climb higher and reach the vistas of our true potential. Such is the journey of life—upward, onward, and always forward."

ppp

SIX

AFFIRMATIONS FOR STRESS RELIEF

Affirmations for stress relief are specifically designed to calm the mind and reduce anxiety by promoting a sense of peace, balance, and control. Stress, a common element of modern life, can significantly impair one's quality of life, affecting both mental and physical health. Effective stress-relief affirmations can help mitigate these effects by fostering a mindset that focuses on tranquility and resilience.

Understanding the Impact of Stress

Stress triggers a cascade of physical and psychological responses that prepare the body to face a perceived threat. However, when stress becomes chronic, it can lead to serious health issues including anxiety, depression, cardiovascular diseases, and a weakened immune system. Managing stress is therefore crucial not only for mental peace but also for maintaining overall health.

The Role of Affirmations in Managing Stress

Affirmations can play a significant role in managing stress by reshaping thought patterns. They help shift focus from stress-inducing thoughts or worries to positive, calming statements that reinforce a sense of well-being and control. Regular use of affirmations as part of stress management can reduce the intensity of stress responses, enhance emotional resilience, and promote a more balanced and peaceful mindset.

Crafting Affirmations for Stress Relief

Creating effective stress-relief affirmations involves focusing on positive outcomes, the presence of peace, and the ability to handle stressors effectively. These affirmations should be tailored to address specific elements that trigger stress in your life and affirm your capability to manage them.

Focus on Peace and Calm: Affirmations should promote a sense of inner peace and calm. Phrases like "I am calm and peaceful in all situations" can help reinforce a tranquil mindset.

Empowerment Against Stressors: It's also beneficial to affirm personal strength in dealing with stress. Statements like "I am equipped to handle any challenges that come my way" empower you to face stressors with confidence.

Positive Outcomes: Affirm the positive outcomes of managing stress well. Use affirmations like "Every deep breath I take calms me and gives me new strength."

Examples of Effective Stress-Relief Affirmations

Here are several affirmations designed to help alleviate stress:

"I am feeling peaceful and centered."

"With every breath, I release the anxiety within me and become more calm."

"I choose to feel calm and peaceful in all situations."

"I have the power to control my stress levels."

"I am letting go of all tensions with each exhale."

"I am surrounded by peace and quiet."

"I embrace tranquility over anxiety."

"My mind is clear, my body is relaxed, and my soul is at peace."

"I possess the qualities needed to be extremely calm and centered."

"I am free from stress and am in sync with the world around me."

Integrating Affirmations into Daily Stress Management

To maximize the effectiveness of these affirmations, integrate them into your daily routine. Consider repeating them during stressful parts of the day, such as during a commute, before a significant meeting, or at moments when stress feels overwhelming. Pairing these affirmations with deep breathing exercises or mindfulness practice can enhance their calming effects.

Consistency and Environment

Consistent use of affirmations can change the way the brain responds to stress over time. For better results, practice your affirmations in a quiet, relaxing environment where you can focus without interruption. This could be a designated relaxation spot in your home or a nature park where you can sit peacefully.

Adapting Affirmations to Changing Needs

As your life changes and evolves, so too might your sources of stress and your responses to them. It is important to continually adapt your affirmations to reflect these changes. Regularly updating and personalizing your affirmations ensures that they remain relevant and effective in providing relief.

Stress-relief affirmations are a simple, effective tool that can help manage and mitigate stress. By focusing on calming the mind, reinforcing personal strength, and cultivating an environment of peace and tranquility, affirmations can transform how you handle stress. Regular practice can lead to significant improvements in your mental well-being and quality of life, empowering you to live more fully and with greater peace.

ϷϷϷ

"The practice of nightly affirmations is like setting
the stage for a peaceful retreat within your mind.
As the body rests, the mind weaves these positive
threads into the subconscious, crafting a tapestry of
calm. By morning, this tapestry becomes a shield,
protecting against the trials of a new day."

☽☽☽

SEVEN

AFFIRMATIONS FOR HEALTHY RELATIONSHIPS

Affirmations for healthy relationships focus on fostering understanding, empathy, and love, which are critical components for nurturing and maintaining strong personal connections. Healthy relationships, whether romantic, familial, or platonic, significantly contribute to our overall well-being and happiness. Through the use of specific affirmations, individuals can cultivate a positive mindset that promotes better communication, deeper understanding, and a more empathetic interaction with others.

The Importance of Healthy Relationships

Relationships play a crucial role in our lives, influencing our mental health, emotional stability, and even our physical well-being. Positive relationships can provide support, enrich our lives, and foster a sense of belonging and community. Conversely, strained relationships can contribute to stress, anxiety, and depression. Therefore, nurturing our relationships through mindful practices such as affirmations can have profound benefits on our holistic health.

How Affirmations Enhance Relationships

Affirmations can serve as powerful tools for relationship enhancement by helping individuals cultivate a positive perspective towards themselves and their interactions with others. They can help reframe negative thoughts and foster an attitude of kindness, generosity, and patience, all of which are essential for healthy relationships.

Crafting Effective Relationship Affirmations

Effective relationship affirmations should focus on the qualities that contribute to strong, healthy relationships. These include communication, patience, understanding, respect, and love. Crafting affirmations that reinforce these qualities can help strengthen the emotional bonds between individuals.

Focus on Open Communication: Affirmations like "I communicate openly and with respect" can encourage more honest and effective communication.

Empathy and Understanding: To enhance empathy, use affirmations such as "I seek to understand and appreciate the perspectives of others."

Commitment to Relationship Growth: Affirmations such as "Every day, I commit to nurturing my relationships" can help maintain the ongoing effort needed to strengthen relationships.

Self-Love and Respect: Healthy relationships start with self-respect and a healthy self-image. Affirmations like "I deserve love and I give love generously" reinforce personal self-worth and the capacity to share that love with others.

Examples of Affirmations for Healthy Relationships

"I am grateful for the love I receive and I return it in abundance."

"I am committed to understanding and meeting the needs of my loved ones."

"I choose to see the best in the people I care about."

"I handle my relationships with love, care, and respect."

"I express my needs and feelings in a loving and respectful manner."

"I am patient and kind in all my personal interactions."

"I am a good listener and I hear what others are truly saying."

"I am supportive and encouraging in my relationships."

"I celebrate the strengths of those around me."

"I offer forgiveness to those who hurt me and embrace peace in our relationship."

Integrating Relationship Affirmations into Daily Life

To make these affirmations part of your daily routine, you might consider repeating them during a morning or evening ritual, or when you are about to interact with a partner or friend. You could also create reminders on your phone or post notes around your home to keep these affirmations top of mind.

Reinforcement through Shared Practice

Sharing affirmations with a partner or family members can also be a powerful way to strengthen relationships. This shared practice not only helps both parties align with the positive aspects of their relationship but also builds a mutual commitment to growth and happiness.

Regular Reflection and Adaptation

As relationships evolve, so too should the affirmations used to nurture them. Regularly reflect on your relationships and update your affirmations to meet new challenges or celebrate growth and achievements. This adaptation keeps the practice relevant and deeply connected to your personal experiences.

The Role of Affirmations in Conflict Resolution

Affirmations can also play a role in conflict resolution by helping to maintain a calm, centered state of mind. Affirmations such as "I approach conflicts with understanding and patience" can prepare you to handle disagreements with composure and empathy, promoting a resolution that is beneficial for all involved.

Affirmations for healthy relationships are a simple yet effective tool for enhancing personal interactions. By focusing on fostering understanding, empathy, and love, these affirmations help create a positive environment that nurtures the growth and deepening of relationships. Regular practice of these affirmations can transform the dynamics of your interactions, making them more fulfilling and harmonious.

ᐱᐱᐱ

"Affirmations for health are whispers to the body, telling it to mend, strengthen, and flourish. Each word is a pulse of energy, guiding the cells in their dance of renewal and repair. In this way, we become conductors of our own symphony of wellness."

ᐅᐅᐅ

EIGHT

AFFIRMATIONS FOR CAREER SUCCESS

Affirmations for career success are aimed at fostering a mindset that enhances professional growth and achievement. In the competitive and often stressful environment of modern workspaces, maintaining a positive and proactive attitude is crucial for career advancement. By using affirmations, professionals can cultivate qualities such as confidence, resilience, and motivation, which are essential for success and fulfillment in their careers.

Understanding the Role of Mindset in Career Success

The mindset with which one approaches career challenges significantly influences outcomes. A positive, growth-oriented mindset can lead to greater opportunities for learning and advancement, while a negative mindset may hinder progress. Affirmations help in building a positive self-image and a belief in one's capabilities, which are vital for taking on new challenges and achieving career goals.

Crafting Effective Career Affirmations

To craft effective career affirmations, it is important to focus on specific goals and the attributes needed to achieve them. These affirmations should be personal, positive, and present tense, expressing the ongoing development and success in your professional life.

Focus on Strengths and Capabilities: Affirmations such as "I am skilled and competent in my work" highlight personal strengths and enhance self-confidence.

Goal-Oriented: Align affirmations with your career goals. For example, if aspiring to a leadership role, use affirmations like "I am an effective and respected leader."

Resilience Against Challenges: To build resilience, affirmations like "I successfully navigate challenges and emerge stronger" can be empowering.

Openness to Opportunities: Affirmations that focus on openness to new opportunities, such as "I attract diverse projects that expand my skills," can encourage a more adventurous and growth-focused career path.

Examples of Affirmations for Career Success

"I am advancing towards my career goals every day."

"I attract success by working smart and staying aligned with my values."

"I am a valued contributor to my team and respected in my profession."

"Every day, I build professional relationships that are beneficial for my career."

"I am constantly learning and evolving within my career."

"I handle work pressures with calmness and efficiency."

"I am confident in my abilities to solve problems and make impactful decisions."

"I embrace new challenges as opportunities for growth."

"I am an excellent communicator and influence my colleagues positively."

"I deserve and receive appreciation for my hard work and dedication."

Integrating Career Affirmations into Daily Life

To effectively utilize career affirmations, integrate them into your daily routine. Recite your affirmations during morning preparations or incorporate them into your professional meditation sessions. You can also use affirmations as motivational pauses during the workday, especially before important meetings or projects.

Enhancing Professional Relationships

Career success is not only about individual achievements but also about building positive relationships within the workplace. Affirmations that focus on teamwork and collaboration, such as "I contribute positively to my team and help bring out the best in us," can improve interactions and strengthen professional networks.

Continuous Learning and Adaptation

In an ever-changing professional landscape, continuous learning and adaptation are key. Affirmations can support this by reinforcing a commitment to growth, such as "I am always adapting and learning from my experiences."

Leveraging Affirmations for Professional Challenges

During times of professional uncertainty or stress, affirmations can provide a stabilizing force. Reaffirming your capabilities and focusing on past successes can help maintain a sense of direction and purpose.

Measuring the Impact of Affirmations

To gauge the effectiveness of career affirmations, regularly reflect on your professional growth and any changes in your attitude towards work. Adjust your affirmations as your career evolves, ensuring they remain relevant and aligned with your goals.

Affirmations for career success are not just about achieving specific professional goals but are also about cultivating a positive, resilient mindset that drives continuous growth and satisfaction. By consistently applying these affirmations, professionals can enhance their performance, adapt to new opportunities, and achieve a fulfilling career trajectory. This proactive approach to career development not only leads to professional success but also contributes to overall personal happiness and well-being.

ppp

"Parenting is an expedition fraught with challenges and triumphs, and affirmations are the compass that guides us through. They remind us to hold fast to patience and empathy, steering us back to the shores of love and understanding when the seas of frustration rise. Thus, we navigate the delicate balance of raising children with grace."

ppp

NINE

Affirmations for Overcoming Fear

Affirmations for overcoming fear focus on fostering courage and resilience, enabling individuals to confront and manage their fears effectively. Fear, a natural emotional response to perceived threats, can be a significant barrier to personal growth and happiness. By using specific affirmations, people can reprogram their mindsets, reducing the impact of fear and enhancing their capacity to act despite it.

Understanding Fear and Its Effects

Fear serves an essential biological function, alerting us to danger and preparing us to deal with it. However, when fears become irrational or disproportionate, they can inhibit actions, decision-making, and overall quality of life. Chronic fear can lead to anxiety, stress, and a host of physical health problems, emphasizing the importance of managing fears appropriately.

Role of Affirmations in Managing Fear

Affirmations can be a powerful tool in the arsenal against fear. They work by gradually reshaping one's thoughts, replacing fearful and negative predictions with positive and empowering beliefs. This cognitive restructuring helps to diminish the psychological power of fear and bolsters one's confidence to face and overcome challenges.

Crafting Effective Fear-Overcoming Affirmations

Effective affirmations for overcoming fear should directly address the fears, be positively framed, and focus on empowerment and courage. They should be specific enough to resonate deeply while being broad enough to cover various situations where fear might arise.

Directly Address Fears: Affirmations like "I face my fears with bravery and openness" directly confront the emotion, reinforcing a proactive attitude towards fear.

Promote Positive Outcomes: Framing affirmations to emphasize positive outcomes helps shift focus from potential dangers to potential successes, such as "I focus on success and find courage to move forward."

Cultivate Self-Belief: To counteract the self-doubt that fear often brings, use affirmations that boost self-esteem and belief in one's capabilities, like "I am competent, smart, and able to handle any situation."

Examples of Affirmations for Overcoming Fear

"I am stronger than my fears and can overcome them."

"Every step I take in facing my fears makes me more courageous."

"I choose to act despite feeling afraid."

"I release all fears and embrace life with enthusiasm."

"I am in control of my fear; it does not control me."

"My courage is stronger than my fear."

"I use my fear as fuel to propel me towards my goals."

"I am safe and supported in all my endeavors."

"I trust in my ability to unlock the way and set myself free."

"Fear is only a feeling; it cannot hold me back."

Integrating Fear-Overcoming Affirmations into Daily Life

To make these affirmations part of your life, consider incorporating them into your daily routines, such as during meditation, journaling, or quiet reflection time. You can also repeat them during moments when you feel fear beginning to surface, using them as a tool to regain control and refocus your mindset.

Overcoming Specific Fears

For individuals dealing with specific fears, such as public speaking or heights, tailored affirmations can be particularly effective. Crafting affirmations that address these specific situations can provide the targeted encouragement needed to face and eventually overcome these fears.

Continuous Practice and Reinforcement

The effectiveness of affirmations increases with consistent practice. Over time, the positive statements become ingrained in your subconscious, slowly altering your underlying beliefs and reducing the instinctive power of fear.

Monitoring Progress and Adapting Affirmations

As you progress in your journey to overcome fear, it's important to regularly reflect on the effectiveness of your affirmations and adapt them as necessary. This might involve modifying the language to better suit your evolving situation or adding new affirmations that address emerging fears or challenges.

Affirmations as Part of a Broader Fear-Management Strategy

While affirmations are a powerful tool for overcoming fear, they are most effective when used in conjunction with other fear-management techniques such as therapy, mindfulness practices, and exposure therapy. This holistic approach ensures that you are not only addressing the symptoms of fear but also its root causes.

Affirmations for overcoming fear are a simple, yet profoundly effective method for transforming fear into courage. They empower individuals to face their fears with confidence and resilience, paving the way for personal growth and fulfillment. Regularly practicing these affirmations can significantly alter how fear is perceived and handled, ultimately leading to a braver, bolder, and more satisfying life.

ppp

"In the workplace, affirmations serve as the undercurrent that propels us toward professional success and fulfillment. They remind us of our capabilities and goals, transforming the mundane into a pursuit of passion and achievement. Every affirmation is a reaffirmation of our potential to lead and innovate."

ᗡᗡᗡ

TEN

AFFIRMATIONS FOR HEALING

Affirmations for healing focus on harnessing the power of positive mental reinforcement to promote both emotional and physical recovery. The concept that the mind can influence the body's healing processes is widely recognized in various psychological and medical fields. Through targeted affirmations, individuals can cultivate a mindset that supports healing, reduces stress, and enhances overall well-being.

Understanding the Healing Power of the Mind

The mind-body connection is a fundamental principle in holistic health practices. It posits that psychological factors can affect physical health and vice versa. Stress, anxiety, and negative thinking can exacerbate physical symptoms and delay recovery. Conversely, a positive outlook can improve physical health outcomes by boosting the immune system, reducing pain, and accelerating recovery. This interconnection highlights the importance of mental attitudes and beliefs in the healing process.

Role of Affirmations in Healing

Affirmations can significantly contribute to healing by shifting thoughts from negative, disease-focused patterns to positive, health-oriented patterns. These positive affirmations reinforce the body's capabilities and the individual's resolve to heal, promoting a beneficial psychological environment for recovery.

Crafting Effective Healing Affirmations

Effective healing affirmations should be positive, present tense, and reflect a belief in the healing process. They should focus on health, well-being, and the body's inherent ability to heal itself.

Positive and Affirmative: Affirmations should always be positive, avoiding any negative connotations or reminders of illness. For example, "I am full of vitality and my body heals quickly" is more effective than "I am no longer sick."

Present Tense: It is crucial to phrase affirmations as though the healing is currently happening. This helps create a mental image of present health, which can influence the subconscious mind more effectively. An example would be "My body is capable and strong, and it heals itself every day."

Focus on the Process: Recognizing and affirming the body's ongoing healing process can reinforce patience and persistence, which are vital during recovery. Affirmations like "Every day, my health improves" can be very supportive.

Examples of Affirmations for Healing

"I am healing deeply and completely."

"Every cell in my body vibrates with energy and health."

"I am surrounded by love and everything is fine."

"My body knows how to heal itself, and is doing so right now."

"My wonderful body is healing beautifully."

"I allow my mind to relax and let the healing energy flow through my body."

"With every breath, I release tension and my body heals."

"I am grateful for my body's innate ability to heal."

"I feel stronger and healthier each day."

"I choose to nourish my body with healthy choices that improve my well-being."

Integrating Healing Affirmations into Daily Life

Incorporating healing affirmations into everyday life can enhance their effectiveness. This can be done through several methods:

Regular Repetition: Repeating affirmations throughout the day helps reinforce their message. You might set reminders to affirm health several times a day, especially during times of stress or discomfort.

Meditation and Visualization: Combining affirmations with meditation enhances focus and relaxation, which can be particularly beneficial for healing. Visualization techniques, where the individual imagines the healing process occurring, can augment the impact of affirmations.

Incorporate into Routine: Integrating affirmations into daily routines, such as while drinking morning tea or during a nightly skincare routine, can make the practice a regular part of life.

Adapting Affirmations to Personal Needs

As every individual's healing journey is unique, personalizing affirmations to reflect one's specific health challenges and recovery goals is essential. Tailoring affirmations not only makes them more relevant but also increases their emotional impact.

Continuous Practice and Reflection

Healing is often a gradual process, and maintaining a routine of positive affirmations can help manage expectations and reduce frustration. Regular reflection on the progress made and adjustments to the affirmations to align with current health conditions can keep the practice relevant and motivating.

Affirmations for healing are a powerful tool in the journey towards both physical and emotional recovery. They harness the profound connection between the mind and body to foster an environment conducive to healing. By focusing on positive, health-affirming statements, individuals can influence their path to recovery, enhancing their resilience and capacity for healing. Regular engagement with personalized, positive affirmations can transform the healing process, leading to faster recovery and a more joyful, health-oriented outlook on life.

ᗞᗞᗞ

"*Forgiveness is the key that unlocks the chains of bitterness and resentment. Through affirmations, we turn this key with gentle yet resolute hands, freeing ourselves to move forward unburdened. This release is not just an act of kindness to others but a profound gift to oneself.*"

ELEVEN

AFFIRMATIONS FOR FINANCIAL ABUNDANCE

Affirmations for financial abundance are designed to cultivate a mindset that attracts prosperity and enhances financial well-being. In the realm of personal finance, mindset plays a crucial role in how individuals approach money management, investment decisions, and overall financial planning. Positive affirmations can help reshape one's financial beliefs and behaviors, promoting a more proactive and optimistic approach to achieving financial goals.

Understanding the Impact of Mindset on Financial Health

The connection between mindset and financial success is well-documented. A positive financial mindset encourages behaviors that lead to saving, investing, and wealth building, whereas a negative mindset can result in patterns that undermine financial stability, such as overspending or financial avoidance. By using affirmations, individuals can start to shift their focus from scarcity to abundance, which in turn motivates actions that enhance financial prosperity.

Crafting Effective Financial Affirmations

Effective financial affirmations should be specific, positive, and formulated in the present tense, creating a sense of current prosperity that can help manifest more of the same. These affirmations reinforce confidence in financial decision-making and a belief in one's ability to generate and manage wealth effectively.

Focus on Abundance: Affirmations should emphasize abundance and prosperity to help shift away from any scarcity mindset. An example might be, "Money flows freely and abundantly into my life."

Promote Wise Financial Management: Besides focusing on abundance, it's important to affirm skills in managing that abundance. "I am wise and thoughtful in managing my wealth" is an affirmation that encourages prudent financial stewardship.

Cultivate Gratitude for Current Prosperity: Recognizing and appreciating current resources can enhance a positive outlook on finances. "I am grateful for the wealth I have, and look forward to more" can be a powerful affirmation.

Examples of Affirmations for Financial Abundance

"I am a magnet for money. Prosperity is drawn to me."

"I constantly attract opportunities that create more money."

"My actions create constant prosperity."

"I am aligned with the energy of abundance."

"I wisely manage my financial success with integrity."

"I am deserving of financial security and am open to all avenues of income."

"I release all negative energy over money."

"Money comes to me easily and effortlessly."

"Every day I live my dream of financial abundance."

"I am thankful for the abundance and prosperity in my life."

Integrating Financial Affirmations into Daily Life

To make financial affirmations effective, integrate them into daily routines. This can be done through meditation, visualization, or saying them aloud each morning or evening. Pairing affirmations with financial planning activities like budgeting or reviewing financial statements can reinforce the connection between the mental shift and practical financial actions.

Visualization Techniques

Visualizing financial success while reciting affirmations can enhance the emotional and psychological impact of those affirmations. Imagine living the life you desire with financial ease—owning a home, traveling, or simply enjoying a debt-free life. This visualization helps solidify the belief in financial abundance.

Regular Review and Adaptation

As financial situations change, so should the affirmations. Regularly updating affirmations to reflect current goals or to adapt to new financial circumstances keeps them relevant and aligned with one's financial reality.

Overcoming Financial Anxiety with Affirmations

Financial affirmations can also play a crucial role in managing financial anxiety. By maintaining a focus on abundance and success, affirmations help mitigate fears around money, which can be a barrier to effective financial management.

Affirmations and Financial Education

While affirmations are powerful, they should be part of a broader financial strategy that includes education, planning, and advice. Understanding financial principles can empower individuals to make informed decisions that bolster the effectiveness of their affirmations.

Affirmations for financial abundance are not just wishful thinking—they are a practical tool for cultivating a prosperous mindset that can lead to tangible financial improvements. By focusing on abundance, effective management, and gratitude, these affirmations help shape a positive financial identity. Regular practice, combined with sound financial strategies, can transform one's financial outlook, leading to enhanced well-being and a more secure financial future.

ppp

"Affirmations in difficult times are like lighthouses in a stormy sea, providing a beacon of hope and strength when we need it most. They remind us that we are not our circumstances; we are the resilience and courage that rise above them. With each affirmation, we declare our power to endure and overcome."

♡♡♡

TWELVE

AFFIRMATIONS FOR PERSONAL GROWTH

Affirmations for personal growth are targeted phrases that foster an environment conducive to continual development and learning. These affirmations are intended to support an individual's journey towards becoming a better, more capable version of themselves. Personal growth involves enhancing various aspects of life, including emotional intelligence, professional skills, personal relationships, and overall mental health. By repeating affirmations focused on growth and learning, individuals can cultivate a mindset that embraces challenges as opportunities for development.

The Importance of Personal Growth

Personal growth is vital for a fulfilling and satisfying life. It contributes to self-awareness, improves resilience, and helps individuals adapt to changes and overcome life's challenges. Continuous personal development is also linked to increased happiness and reduced stress, as it promotes a proactive approach to life and its obstacles.

Crafting Affirmations for Personal Growth

Effective affirmations for personal growth should be focused, positive, and framed in the present tense. They should resonate with the individual's personal aspirations and be relevant to the areas of life where growth is desired.

Emphasize Progress and Learning: Affirmations like "Every day, I learn something new and grow in my abilities" highlight continuous improvement and the value of learning.

Encourage Openness and Flexibility: To foster adaptability, use affirmations that promote openness to new experiences, such as "I embrace change and adapt to it with ease."

Support Self-Acceptance and Self-Compassion: Since personal growth also involves understanding and accepting oneself, affirmations like "I am patient with myself and accept myself as I am while striving to improve" are beneficial.

Examples of Affirmations for Personal Growth

"I am committed to personal growth and welcome the lessons that shape me."

"I am constantly evolving, learning, and improving."

"I allow myself to move out of my comfort zone to grow."

"I am dedicated to developing more positive and empowering habits."

"Every challenge I face is an opportunity to grow and learn."

"I am a lifelong learner, always eager to expand my understanding and knowledge."

"I treat myself with compassion and respect, knowing that personal growth involves time and patience."

"I actively seek new experiences that challenge my perspectives and enhance my skills."

"I am grateful for my journey and every experience that contributes to my growth."

"I acknowledge my strengths and work on my weaknesses to become a well-rounded individual."

Integrating Personal Growth Affirmations into Daily Life

Integrating affirmations into everyday routines can magnify their impact. This could include reciting them during morning meditation, writing them in a journal, or reflecting on them during moments of quiet throughout the day. Consistently reminding oneself of the commitment to growth helps keep this goal present and active in daily life.

Continuous Learning and Improvement

Using affirmations to stay committed to continuous learning and self-improvement can create a positive feedback loop. As individuals experience the benefits of growth, such as increased confidence and competence, the affirmations reinforce the value of these experiences, encouraging further development.

Overcoming Barriers with Affirmations

Personal growth can sometimes be hindered by fears, self-doubt, or past failures. Affirmations can help overcome these barriers by reinforcing a sense of capability and worth. Phrases like "I am capable of overcoming any setbacks" or "I learn valuable lessons from all experiences" can diminish the impact of past negatives and foster a resilient and optimistic outlook.

Regular Review and Adaptation of Affirmations

As personal goals and circumstances evolve, so too should the affirmations. Regularly updating affirmations to align with current challenges and aspirations ensures they remain relevant and supportive.

The Role of Affirmations in a Balanced Life

Affirmations for personal growth also support a balanced approach to life, reminding individuals to nurture not just professional and intellectual aspects, but also emotional and spiritual facets. This holistic approach to growth is crucial for sustained well-being and effectiveness.

Affirmations for personal growth are a powerful tool in the pursuit of continual development. They help cultivate a mindset that values learning and self-improvement, encouraging individuals to embrace new challenges and opportunities for growth. Regularly engaging with personal growth affirmations can lead to significant improvements in how individuals view themselves and their potential, ultimately leading to a more enriched and purposeful life.

ϷϷϷ

"Financial affirmations are the currency of belief, investing in the wealth of our own potential. They teach us to value ourselves and expect abundance, setting the stage for prosperity to flow into our lives. This mindset of wealth attracts opportunities and opens doors previously unseen."

THIRTEEN

AFFIRMATIONS FOR HAPPINESS

Affirmations for happiness focus on fostering a consistent sense of joy and contentment in daily life. These affirmations help cultivate a mindset that prioritizes positivity, appreciation, and satisfaction, which are key components of a happy life. By consciously choosing to affirm happiness, individuals can influence their emotional state, enhance their overall well-being, and find greater fulfillment in their everyday experiences.

Understanding the Role of Mindset in Happiness

The mindset with which one approaches life greatly influences their overall happiness. A mindset oriented towards gratitude, optimism, and positivity is more likely to experience joy and contentment. Psychological research supports the idea that happiness is not just a result of external circumstances but also a product of our mental habits and attitudes. Affirmations can play a significant role in shaping these attitudes, encouraging a focus on the positives in life and cultivating resilience against negativity.

Crafting Effective Happiness Affirmations

Effective happiness affirmations should be personal, positive, and present tense. They should focus on appreciating the present moment, recognizing the good in life, and fostering an attitude of gratitude.

Emphasize Present Enjoyment: Affirmations like "I find joy in every moment" encourage an appreciation for the present, regardless of the situation.

Cultivate Gratitude: Gratitude is a powerful enhancer of happiness. Affirmations such as "I am grateful for every day and all it brings" help maintain a positive focus.

Promote Positive Framing: To cultivate a habit of seeing the good in every situation, use affirmations like "I always find something to smile about."

Examples of Affirmations for Happiness

"I embrace happiness as my set state of being."

"I am filled with joy and gratitude for my life."

"Happiness flows freely from me and to me."

"I find joy and pleasure in the simplest things in life."

"Every day I discover more of what makes me happy."

"I choose to be happy right now. I love my life."

"I spread joy with every step I take on my journey."

"I am responsible for my happiness and I create it with love."

"My heart is overflowing with joy."

"I face each day with a smile and a heart full of gratitude."

Integrating Happiness Affirmations into Daily Life

To effectively utilize happiness affirmations, integrate them into daily routines such as morning meditations, during breaks at work, or in the evening before bed. The consistent repetition of these affirmations helps them become ingrained in the subconscious, making happiness a more automatic state.

Visualization Techniques

Pairing affirmations with visualization can enhance their impact. Visualizing oneself in a happy state while reciting affirmations can reinforce the feelings they are meant to evoke. This practice helps bridge the gap between mere words and actual emotions, making the affirmations more powerful.

Overcoming Challenges with Affirmations

Life's inevitable challenges can sometimes overshadow happiness. Affirmations can serve as a tool for resilience, reminding individuals to find joy even in difficult times. Affirmations like "I choose happiness, especially in challenging times" reinforce the ability to maintain positivity in the face of adversity.

Continuous Practice and Reflection

The effectiveness of happiness affirmations increases with regular practice. Reflecting on the joy these affirmations bring and adapting them to fit changing life circumstances can help maintain their relevance and power.

Sharing Happiness

Happiness is often magnified when shared. Using affirmations to not only boost personal happiness but also to spread it to others can create a positive feedback loop in social environments. Affirmations like "I bring joy to those around me" encourage a socially expansive approach to happiness.

The Broader Impact of Happiness Affirmations

Beyond individual benefits, happiness affirmations can have a broader impact on one's life, influencing relationships, work performance, and overall health. The positive emotions generated by these affirmations can improve social interactions, increase productivity, and enhance physical well-being.

Affirmations for happiness are a vital tool for anyone seeking to enhance their joy in life. By focusing on the positives, cultivating gratitude, and maintaining a joyful mindset through affirmations, individuals can significantly improve their emotional and overall life satisfaction. Regular engagement with happiness affirmations allows for a deeper appreciation of life's gifts and a fuller, more joyful experience of everyday living.

ᗡᗡᗡ

"Affirmations for happiness teach us to cherish each
moment and find joy in the smallest of blessings.
They rewire our thoughts to celebrate the present
and anticipate the future with optimism. It is in
this state of gratitude that true happiness
flourishes."

♥♥♥

FOURTEEN

AFFIRMATIONS FOR FORGIVENESS

Affirmations for forgiveness are vital tools for releasing past hurts and embracing a mindset of reconciliation and peace. Forgiveness is a powerful process that not only heals old wounds but also clears the path for personal growth and healthier relationships. By using affirmations, individuals can facilitate this healing process, allowing themselves to move beyond the pain and resentment that often linger after being wronged.

The Importance of Forgiveness

Forgiveness is essential for emotional health because it allows individuals to let go of negative emotions that can be harmful if held onto for too long. These negative emotions include anger, bitterness, and a desire for revenge, all of which can consume a lot of emotional energy and detract from overall happiness. Moreover, holding onto grievances can lead to chronic stress, which negatively affects the body, contributing to issues like high blood pressure, heart disease, and a weakened immune system.

Understanding Forgiveness

Forgiveness does not mean condoning or excusing wrongdoing, nor does it necessitate reconciliation with the person who caused the harm. Instead, forgiveness is about finding peace for oneself, releasing the grip of negative feelings, and moving forward with greater wisdom and understanding.

Crafting Effective Forgiveness Affirmations

Effective forgiveness affirmations should focus on releasing the past, healing emotional wounds, and opening up to the possibility of new, positive experiences. These affirmations should be framed positively, expressed in the present tense, and be personally meaningful.

Release and Let Go: Affirmations such as "I release the past and forgive everyone, including myself" help in letting go of old grievances.

Self-Compassion and Understanding: Since forgiveness can sometimes include forgiving oneself, affirmations like "I treat myself with kindness and forgiveness" are crucial.

Embracing Peace: To promote a peaceful mindset, use affirmations like "I choose peace over resentment."

Examples of Affirmations for Forgiveness

"I forgive myself and others, and I release the burden of being hurt."

"I am capable of moving beyond past hurts to embrace healing and love."

"I let go of resentment now and fill my heart with peace."

"I forgive those who have harmed me in the past and peacefully detach from them."

"Forgiveness frees me and allows me to live in a state of love."

"I am a forgiving and loving person, and I accept the flaws in others."

"I choose to forgive, as it brings me inner peace and joy."

"With each breath, I release anger and invite forgiveness into my heart."

"I am strong enough to forgive, and this strength creates a happier future for me."

"I embrace the freedom that comes with forgiveness."

Integrating Forgiveness Affirmations into Daily Life

Integrating forgiveness affirmations into daily life can enhance their effectiveness. This might include reciting them during meditation, before sleep, or at moments when old resentments tend to surface. Regular repetition helps to embed these healing thoughts into the subconscious, making forgiveness a more automatic response.

The Healing Power of Forgiveness

The act of forgiving can be profoundly healing. It not only resolves old emotional wounds but also improves mental health by reducing anxiety, depression, and hostility. People who forgive also tend to have better self-esteem and more enjoyable relationships.

Continuous Practice and Adaptation

As with any emotional healing process, the journey of forgiveness is ongoing. It may require regular revisiting and reaffirmation, especially when old feelings resurface or new grievances occur. Continuously practicing forgiveness affirmations helps to maintain a forgiving attitude and ensures emotional resilience.

Challenges in Forgiveness

Forgiving is not always easy, especially when the emotional wounds are deep or the actions against one have been particularly hurtful. It's important to recognize that forgiveness is a process that can require time and patience. During this process, affirmations serve as gentle reminders of one's commitment to healing and personal peace.

Broader Impacts of Practicing Forgiveness

Practicing forgiveness has broader implications for one's overall well-being. It can lead to improved mental and physical health, enhanced relationships, and even greater spiritual satisfaction. Those who embrace forgiveness often find that they are happier, more compassionate, and more open to positive experiences.

Affirmations for forgiveness are powerful tools in the healing process, helping individuals to release past hurts and embrace a future marked by peace and emotional freedom. By consistently applying these affirmations, individuals can foster a more forgiving attitude, enhancing their emotional well-being and leading to a more fulfilling life.

ୡୡୡ

"Learning through affirmations is an education of the soul, a curriculum written in the language of positivity and growth. Each lesson reinforces our innate strengths and encourages us to rise above our perceived limitations. Education, after all, is not just about acquiring knowledge but about transforming ourselves."

❦❦❦

FIFTEEN

NIGHT-TIME AFFIRMATIONS FOR PEACEFUL SLEEP

Nighttime affirmations are designed to calm the mind and prepare the body for a restful sleep, making them a crucial element of a healthy nighttime routine. Sleep is vital for physical health, emotional balance, and cognitive performance, but many struggle with sleep disturbances due to stress, anxiety, or other disruptions. By incorporating affirmations into one's evening routine, individuals can create a conducive environment for sleep, characterized by peace and tranquility.

The Importance of Quality Sleep

Quality sleep is essential for the body to repair itself and for the brain to consolidate memories and process information. Lack of sleep can lead to a host of problems, including impaired cognitive function, increased stress response, weight gain, and a weakened immune system. Therefore, creating practices that promote adequate and quality sleep is crucial for overall health.

Understanding Nighttime Affirmations

Nighttime affirmations are positive statements that are meant to be recited or contemplated upon before sleep. Their purpose is to replace the day's stress and worries with positive and calming thoughts. These affirmations help quiet the mind, reduce anxiety, and set the tone for a deep and rejuvenating sleep.

Crafting Effective Nighttime Affirmations

Effective nighttime affirmations should focus on relaxation, release of the day's burdens, and the nurturing of positive feelings. They should be simple, positive, and in the present tense to maximize their calming effect.

Promote Relaxation: Affirmations such as "My body is relaxed and ready for sleep" help soothe the physical body and prepare it for rest.

Encourage Mental Release: To mentally disconnect from the day's stresses, affirmations like "I release all thoughts of the day and welcome rest" can be beneficial.

Cultivate Positive Emotional States: Affirmations that promote feelings of gratitude and contentment, such as "I am grateful for the day and happily look forward to tomorrow," enhance emotional well-being at bedtime.

Examples of Nighttime Affirmations for Peaceful Sleep

"I am calm and peaceful as I lay down to sleep."

"Each breath I take deepens my relaxation."

"My mind is clear, my body is rested, and I welcome sleep."

"I let go of all the worries of the day; my sleep is deep and refreshing."

"With every night, my sleep becomes more peaceful."

"I am thankful for this day and release it with love."

"I embrace the silence of the night and know that I am safe."

"Sleep comes naturally to me and my dreams are soothing."

"I am surrounded by peace. My sleep is restful."

"I end this day with peace and start tomorrow with strength."

Integrating Nighttime Affirmations into Daily Life

Incorporating nighttime affirmations can be done through several methods. One might recite them silently while lying in bed, or say them aloud during a pre-sleep meditation session. Writing affirmations in a journal before bed can also help manifest these calming thoughts.

The Role of a Relaxing Environment

Creating a relaxing environment that supports the effectiveness of nighttime affirmations is essential. This might include dimming the lights, reducing noise, or using aromatherapy with calming scents like lavender. The physical environment should encourage relaxation to complement the mental relaxation promoted by the affirmations.

Addressing Sleep Anxiety

For those who suffer from sleep anxiety or insomnia, nighttime affirmations can be particularly helpful. By focusing the mind on positive, reassuring thoughts, affirmations can reduce the anxiety that often prevents sleep.

Regular Practice and Adaptation

The benefits of nighttime affirmations increase with regular use. Making them a part of every evening routine can help condition the mind and body to associate these affirmations with the onset of sleep. Over time, merely starting the routine may begin to trigger a relaxation response.

Broader Benefits of Restful Sleep

Beyond the immediate benefit of improved sleep quality, nighttime affirmations can influence daytime energy levels, mood, and overall health. A good night's sleep supported by positive affirmations can lead to a more productive, joyful, and healthy life.

Nighttime affirmations for peaceful sleep are not just a tool for ending the day but are a critical component of a holistic approach to health and well-being. By focusing on relaxation, release, and positivity at bedtime, individuals can significantly improve their sleep quality and, by extension, their overall quality of life. Regularly practicing these affirmations can transform nighttime into a period of peaceful restoration, setting the stage for a successful and vibrant tomorrow.

ቅቅቅ

"In the silent moments before sleep, affirmations become the soothing melody that lulls the mind into tranquility. They are the gentle closure to the day's chaos, inviting restorative sleep to heal and rejuvenate. This nightly ritual is a renewal of both body and spirit."

ᚦᚦᚦ

SIXTEEN

AFFIRMATIONS IN DIFFICULT TIMES

Affirmations in difficult times are essential tools for maintaining mental strength and positivity. When faced with challenges, whether personal crises, professional setbacks, or broader uncertainties, the mind can easily spiral into negativity and despair. Affirmations provide a counterbalance to these tendencies, promoting resilience, optimism, and the mental fortitude necessary to navigate through tough periods.

The Role of Affirmations During Challenges

Difficult times often trigger a fight-or-flight response, which can cloud judgment and lead to impulsive decisions or overwhelming feelings of despair. Affirmations serve as gentle yet powerful reminders that help center the mind, foster stability, and encourage a more balanced perspective. They reinforce the individual's capacity to handle adversity and instill a sense of control and hope.

Crafting Effective Affirmations for Difficult Times

To be effective during tough times, affirmations should be direct, comforting, and empowering. They should reinforce the individual's inner strength, adaptability, and the transient nature of most challenges.

Focus on Strength and Resilience: Affirmations like "I am stronger than my challenges" empower individuals to draw upon their inner reserves of strength.

Encourage Perspective: Phrases such as "This is temporary, and I will come out stronger" help maintain a long-term perspective, which is crucial during transient difficulties.

Promote Positive Outcomes: Using affirmations that visualize positive outcomes, like "Every step I take is towards a brighter future," can motivate forward movement even when the path seems unclear.

Examples of Affirmations for Difficult Times

"I am resilient, strong, and brave enough to overcome this."

"I choose to find hopeful and optimistic ways to look at this."

"I am equipped to handle whatever comes my way."

"This challenge will only make me stronger and wiser."

"I trust in my ability to navigate through this difficult time."

"I am patient with myself and understand that great things take time."

"I find strength in my struggles and am learning every day."

"My spirit is unbreakable, and I am built to withstand hardships."

"I embrace this challenge as an opportunity to grow and learn."

"I am surrounded by support, both seen and unseen."

Integrating Affirmations into Daily Life During Challenges

Integrating affirmations into daily routines is particularly crucial during difficult times. These can be recited during meditation, written in a journal, or repeated mentally during stressful moments. Many find it helpful to post these affirmations in visible places—such as on a bathroom mirror or computer monitor—to serve as constant reminders of their resilience and strength.

The Power of Routine and Consistency

Maintaining a routine that includes daily affirmations can provide a sense of normalcy and control amid chaos. Consistency in these practices not only reinforces their positive messages but also structures the day in a way that supports mental health and emotional stability.

Overcoming Mental Barriers with Affirmations

During challenging times, mental barriers such as doubt and fear can significantly impede progress. Affirmations help break down these barriers by continuously reinforcing a narrative of capability and positivity, which is essential for overcoming the paralysis that fear and doubt can create.

Adapting Affirmations to Changing Circumstances

As situations evolve, so too should the affirmations. Tailoring affirmations to address specific aspects of current challenges can enhance their effectiveness and relevance, providing targeted support as needed.

Broader Implications of Using Affirmations

Beyond individual benefits, using affirmations during difficult times can also improve interpersonal relationships by reducing stress responses that might otherwise strain interactions. They contribute to a healthier mental environment, facilitating better communication and more empathetic interactions.

Affirmations in difficult times are not just tools for coping but are essential elements of mental and emotional resilience. They fortify the spirit, clarify the mind, and prepare the individual for the daily challenges of navigating adversity. Regularly practicing these affirmations cultivates an inner strength that is capable of facing not just current difficulties, but any of life's challenges, with courage and positivity. Through sustained use, these affirmations can transform the way individuals perceive and react to challenges, leading to more effective coping strategies and a more optimistic outlook on life.

❧❧❧

"Sharing affirmations is a ritual of connection,
binding individuals through shared aspirations
and collective strength. In this shared space,
affirmations become more than personal
mantras—they are the echoes of a community's
heartbeat. Together, we find courage and comfort in
the shared pursuit of a better self."

SEVENTEEN

AFFIRMATIONS FOR PHYSICAL HEALTH

Affirmations for physical health are designed to promote health, vitality, and overall well-being through the power of positive thinking. The connection between the mind and body is profound, with countless studies demonstrating how positive mental attitudes can influence physical health outcomes. By using specific affirmations, individuals can encourage their bodies towards better health and foster a greater sense of vitality.

The Connection Between Mind and Body

The mind-body connection highlights the impact that thoughts and emotions have on physical health. Positive mental states can boost the immune system, improve recovery times, and reduce the risk of numerous diseases by managing stress and promoting healthier lifestyle choices. Affirmations serve as tools to harness this connection, focusing the mind on health and wellness which in turn influences the body to maintain and improve its condition.

Crafting Effective Health Affirmations

Effective health affirmations should be specific, encouraging, and framed in the present tense to enhance their impact. They should foster a sense of health that is already being experienced, not something that is distant or uncertain.

Focus on Current Health: Affirmations like "I am full of energy and vitality" emphasize the existing aspects of health and well-being.

Encourage Positive Health Behaviors: Phrases such as "I nourish my body with healthy food" can promote actions that contribute to physical health.

Support Recovery and Healing: For those recovering from illness or managing chronic conditions, affirmations like "Every day, my body becomes stronger and more resilient" can be particularly powerful.

Examples of Affirmations for Physical Health

"My body is capable of healing, and every day it gets stronger."

"I am surrounded by love and everything I do contributes to my healthy living."

"I give my body the care and nourishment it deserves."

"My sleep is relaxed and refreshing, and I wake up feeling revitalized."

"I listen to my body's needs and honor them."

"I am grateful for my body's innate ability to heal itself."

"Every cell in my body vibrates with energy and health."

"I breathe deeply, exercise regularly, and feed my body nutritious food."

"I love every part of my body and celebrate its strength and vitality."

"I am committed to keeping my mind and body healthy."

Integrating Physical Health Affirmations into Daily Life

Incorporating affirmations for physical health into daily routines can enhance their effectiveness. This could involve reciting them during a morning workout, while preparing a healthy meal, or during meditation and yoga practices. Consistent reinforcement helps solidify these health-positive messages in the mind, which can then influence the body's health behaviors and states.

Visualization Techniques

Pairing affirmations with visualization can amplify their effects. Visualizing oneself as healthy, vibrant, and active while reciting affirmations can enhance the mind-body connection, making the affirmations more potent. This technique can be particularly useful for those recovering from illness or striving to achieve significant health goals.

The Role of Routine and Consistency

Maintaining a routine that includes daily affirmations helps create a constant reinforcement of health and vitality. Consistency is key in shifting long-term thinking patterns and establishing new, health-promoting habits.

Overcoming Health Challenges with Affirmations

Affirmations can also be tailored to address specific health challenges, such as chronic pain or long-term illnesses. In these cases, affirmations focusing on pain management and healing can provide psychological and emotional support that complements medical treatments.

Regular Review and Adaptation of Affirmations

As health conditions change, so too should the affirmations. It is important to adjust affirmations to reflect new health goals, achievements, or setbacks, keeping them relevant and personally meaningful.

Broader Benefits of Health Affirmations

Beyond impacting physical health directly, health affirmations can also encourage a more active lifestyle, healthier eating habits, and improved mental health. These broader benefits can lead to an enhanced quality of life and greater long-term health outcomes.

Affirmations for physical health are powerful tools that can influence not only the mental but also the physical realm, promoting health, vitality, and overall well-being. By regularly engaging with positive affirmations focused on health, individuals can foster a more proactive attitude towards their health, support their healing and recovery processes, and enhance their overall life satisfaction through improved physical condition. Through sustained practice, these affirmations help individuals achieve a healthier, more vibrant life, fully harnessing the mind-body connection.

ᗅᗅᗅ

"Affirmations remind us that the journey of
personal growth is continuous and ever-evolving.
They are the signposts along the path that
encourage us to keep moving forward, even when
the destination feels far away. With each step, we
are closer than we think."

♡♡♡

EIGHTEEN

AFFIRMATIONS FOR PARENTING

Affirmations for parenting are designed to support mothers and parents in their challenging yet rewarding roles. Parenting can often be both physically and emotionally demanding, and maintaining a positive and resilient mindset is crucial. Through the use of affirmations, parents can cultivate patience, understanding, and strength, enhancing their ability to raise happy, healthy, and confident children.

The Role of Affirmations in Parenting

Parenting requires a myriad of skills, including patience, compassion, discipline, and unconditional love. Affirmations can reinforce these qualities, helping parents to stay grounded and centered even amidst the chaos of daily life with children. They can also help to alleviate common feelings of inadequacy or frustration that many parents experience, reinforcing their confidence and competence in their parenting skills.

Crafting Effective Parenting Affirmations

Effective parenting affirmations should focus on the personal qualities and values important for successful parenting. They should be positive, present tense, and resonate emotionally with the parent using them.

Promote Patience and Understanding: Affirmations like "I am patient and understanding with my children" help reinforce these essential qualities.

Encourage Positive Interactions: To foster positive interactions with children, use affirmations such as "I communicate with my child in a loving and respectful manner."

Support Personal Well-being: Parenting can be draining, so affirmations should also focus on the parent's well-being, such as "I take care of my own needs to be the best parent I can be."

Examples of Affirmations for Parenting

"I am a loving and caring parent, and I show this in all my actions."

"Every day, I strive to be the best parent I can be."

"I listen to my children with understanding and without judgment."

"I am grateful for the joys and challenges of parenting."

"My children appreciate and love me, even when we have difficult days."

"I am patient, even in the midst of chaos."

"I teach my children confidence and self-respect by modeling these qualities myself."

"I respond to my children with love and understanding, even when it is hard."

"I am strong and resilient, well-equipped to meet the demands of parenting."

"My bond with my children grows stronger and deeper each day."

Integrating Parenting Affirmations into Daily Life

Integrating affirmations into daily parenting routines can make them more effective. Parents might recite affirmations during quiet moments in the morning before the children wake up, or silently repeat them during challenging interactions with their children. Posting them on the refrigerator, bathroom mirror, or in the car can also serve as helpful reminders throughout the day.

The Power of Positive Modeling

Affirmations not only benefit the parent but also model positive mental habits for children. By hearing and observing their parents use affirmations, children learn the importance of positive thinking and self-compassion, skills that are beneficial throughout life.

Addressing Parental Stress

Parenting can often be stressful, and affirmations can be a tool to manage this stress effectively. They help maintain a perspective that emphasizes growth and joy, rather than the difficulties of parenting.

Regular Practice and Reflection

For affirmations to be most effective, they should be part of a regular practice. Reflecting on the day's parenting successes and challenges can help refine the affirmations used, making them more relevant and powerful.

Broader Impacts of Parenting Affirmations

Beyond improving individual interactions, parenting affirmations can enhance the overall family dynamics. They promote a more positive home environment, reduce stress, and improve communication between family members.

Aaffirmations for parenting are a valuable tool for mothers and parents striving to meet the demands of raising children with grace and resilience. These affirmations help nurture not only the children's well-being but also that of the parents. By regularly employing these positive statements, parents can enhance their effectiveness, reduce stress, and create a loving and supportive family environment. This practice not only enriches the lives of the individuals within the family but also strengthens the family unit as a whole, fostering a nurturing, supportive, and positive home life.

ৡৡৡ

"Each affirmation is a brushstroke in the masterpiece of our lives. With bold colors of confidence and broad strokes of purpose, we paint our future. This creative process is personal, powerful, and perpetually in motion."

♡♡♡

NINETEEN

THE ROLE OF COMMUNITY IN AFFIRMATIONS

Affirmations, typically seen as a personal tool for self-improvement and empowerment, also hold significant communal benefits when shared within a group or community. The role of community in affirmations can greatly amplify their impact, helping to strengthen bonds among individuals and fostering an atmosphere of mutual support and encouragement. This communal aspect of affirmations can transform them from isolated exercises into powerful social interactions that promote collective well-being and cohesion.

Understanding the Communal Power of Affirmations

While affirmations are often practiced individually, their communal use can extend their benefits beyond personal boundaries, influencing group dynamics and enhancing social connections. When people share affirmations, they not only reinforce their personal beliefs and goals but also create shared experiences that can deepen relationships and build trust among members of a community.

Crafting Community-Centric Affirmations

Effective communal affirmations should be inclusive, positive, and reflect common goals or values. They should be designed to resonate with all members of the community, supporting not only individual aspirations but also fostering a sense of collective purpose.

Emphasize Collective Strengths and Goals: Affirmations like "Together, we grow stronger and overcome all challenges" highlight the power of collective effort and mutual support.

Promote Shared Values: To reinforce communal bonds, use affirmations that reflect shared values, such as "We value and respect each other's voices and contributions."

Encourage Unity and Cooperation: Affirmations that focus on unity, like "We are united in our diversity and stronger for it," can help foster a sense of belonging and togetherness.

Examples of Community-Centric Affirmations

"We thrive by supporting one another and celebrating our successes together."

"Each member of our community brings unique value, and together, we create something beautiful."

"We are committed to mutual respect and understanding, which are the foundations of our community."

"Together, we face challenges with courage and optimism."

"Our community is a place of welcome and warmth for everyone."

"We build each other up and believe in the potential of every member."

"Our unity makes us resilient in the face of adversity."

"We share our joys and our struggles, knowing that we are not alone."

"Our collective efforts create positive change that echoes beyond our community."

"We cultivate an environment where all can flourish and grow."

Integrating Affirmations into Community Activities

Incorporating affirmations into community activities can enhance their effectiveness and the sense of camaraderie within the group. This might include starting meetings with a communal affirmation, creating affirmation-themed community events, or setting up workshops where members can create personal and group affirmations together.

The Role of Leadership in Community Affirmations

Leaders within communities play a crucial role in integrating affirmations into the communal fabric. By modeling the use of affirmations and encouraging their use among community members, leaders can help cultivate a positive atmosphere that promotes shared growth and well-being.

Addressing Community Challenges with Affirmations

Communities often face challenges that can strain social bonds, such as conflicts, economic hardships, or societal changes.

Affirmations can serve as a unifying force during these times, providing a common platform for expression and mutual understanding.

Continuous Practice and Community Development

For affirmations to become a meaningful part of community life, they require regular practice and reinforcement. Community leaders can facilitate this by incorporating affirmations into regular community interactions and making them a staple of community culture.

Broader Impacts of Communal Affirmations

Beyond improving community dynamics, affirmations can have broader social implications. They can enhance social resilience, promote collective action towards common goals, and improve the overall social fabric of larger communities. Affirmations shared within communities can ripple outwards, influencing broader societal attitudes and fostering a more positive, cohesive social environment.

The role of community in affirmations extends the benefits of this practice from the individual to the collective. By sharing affirmations, communities can strengthen their bonds, support one another in personal and communal growth, and create a more positive, unified, and resilient environment. This communal practice not only enriches the lives of individual members but also enhances the collective well-being, making it a powerful tool for community development and social harmony.

ϷϷϷ

"The beauty of affirmations lies in their ability to transform intention into action. They are not just wishes; they are declarations of our active pursuit of happiness, health, and prosperity. With every repeated phrase, we draw our dreams closer to reality."

❦❦❦

TWENTY

Maintaining a Daily Affirmation Practice

Maintaining a daily affirmation practice is essential for harnessing the long-term benefits of affirmations, such as increased positivity, improved self-esteem, and greater resilience in the face of challenges. Integrating affirmations into daily routines not only helps to reinforce these positive messages but also ensures they become a part of one's subconscious, influencing thoughts and behaviors continuously.

Understanding the Benefits of Daily Affirmation Practice

Daily affirmation practice supports the conditioning of the mind towards positive thinking and self-empowerment. This regular practice can significantly influence mental health, reduce stress, and enhance overall life satisfaction by consistently aligning thoughts with desired outcomes and behaviors.

Setting a Routine for Daily Affirmations

Establishing a routine is crucial for the success of any daily practice. For affirmations, this means selecting specific times and settings that support reflection and repetition.

Choose the Right Time: Many find it beneficial to practice affirmations at the start of the day to set a positive tone or at the end of the day to reflect on and affirm positive thoughts before sleep.

Consistent Setting: Consistency in the environment can also aid in forming the habit. Whether it's in front of a mirror, during a morning walk, or in a quiet space, the key is to find a place where you feel comfortable and undisturbed.

Crafting Effective Affirmations

To maximize the benefits of affirmations, they should be personally meaningful, positively framed, and specific. The affirmations should resonate with your core values and goals and be expressed in the present tense to emphasize current and active participation in the desired state or behavior.

Personal Relevance: Make sure the affirmations are directly related to your personal aspirations, challenges, or values. This relevance makes the practice more impactful and meaningful.

Positivity and Clarity: Affirmations should be clear and exclusively positive, focusing on what you want to achieve or feel, rather than what you want to avoid.

Incorporating Affirmations into Daily Activities

To ensure that affirmations are a consistent part of your routine, integrate them into daily activities:

Morning Routine: Start the day with affirmations while brushing your teeth, showering, or having breakfast.

Daily Commute: Use affirmations during your commute by listening to recorded affirmations or repeating them silently.

Meal Times: Pause before meals to affirm something positive, linking the practice to another habitual part of your day.

Exercise Sessions: Incorporate affirmations into your physical exercise routine, which can enhance the physical and mental benefits of both activities.

Using Technology to Support Affirmation Practice

Technology can be a valuable tool in maintaining a daily affirmation practice. Use smartphone apps designed for affirmations, set reminders to affirm throughout the day, or use wallpapers and alarms labeled with affirmations.

Tracking Progress and Reflecting

Keep a journal of your affirmations and reflect on the changes you notice in your thoughts, feelings, and behaviors. This reflection can help you fine-tune your affirmations and deepen your understanding of their effects.

Journaling: Write down your daily affirmations and any reflections or reactions they provoke. This can enhance your awareness of their impact over time.

Adapting Affirmations to Changing Needs

As your life situations and personal growth evolve, so too should your affirmations. Regularly update and adapt your affirmations to reflect current challenges, achievements, and goals. This keeps the practice relevant and effectively supportive of your personal development.

Social Sharing and Community Support

Sharing affirmations with friends, family, or a dedicated group can enhance the practice through mutual encouragement and accountability. This social aspect can also deepen the impact of the affirmations by embedding them within your social interactions and relationships.

Long-Term Integration

For affirmations to truly embed themselves in your subconscious and influence your life positively, they need to be part of a long-term, consistent practice. This ongoing commitment can transform temporary gains into lasting changes.

Maintaining a daily affirmation practice is a profoundly effective way to foster continuous personal growth and well-being. By integrating affirmations into daily routines, actively reflecting on their impact, and adapting them to ongoing personal development, individuals can achieve sustained benefits, enhancing their mental, emotional, and even physical health over time.

ﬢﬢﬢ

"Through the practice of affirmations, we teach ourselves to see not just what is but what can be. This vision is the essence of hope and the foundation of change. It is a vision that guides us, a light that never dims, regardless of the darkness that surrounds us."

♥♥♥

Citation And References

This book represents the culmination of extensive research and meticulous analysis, incorporating a diverse range of sources, including numerous books, scholarly studies, and personal experiences. Additionally, I have scoured various websites to gather relevant information and data essential for the compilation of this work. I have taken every precaution to ensure the accuracy of the information presented and have diligently cited all sources to acknowledge their contributions.

Despite these efforts, the possibility of inadvertent errors remains. I deeply value the insights of my readers and appreciate any feedback that can help identify and rectify such inaccuracies. I encourage you to bring any discrepancies to my attention.

Your feedback is not only welcome but crucial, as it will aid in correcting current editions and enhancing the content of future ones. I am committed to maintaining the highest standards of accuracy and reliability in my work and thank you for your support and understanding.

Additionally, I firmly uphold the principle of freedom of speech and expression as guaranteed under Article 19(1)(a) of the Constitution of India, and I respect the diverse viewpoints and expressions of all readers.

ԿԿԿ

Other Books Of The Author

1. Empowering Minds: A Journey into Women's Self-Discovery and Power
2. The Dynamics of Motivation: Catalyzing Thought into Action
3. Meditation and Mental Well Being: The Path to Inner Peace and Clarity
4. The Psychology of Child Education: Nurturing Future Generations
5. Ethical Enlightenment: A Modern Guide to Living with Integrity
6. Voices of Empowerment: Stories of Women Rising Against Odds
7. Social Psychology in Everyday Life: Understanding Human Connections
8. The Essence of Motivational Speaking: Inspiring Change in Others
9. Balancing Acts: Women, Work, and the Will to Lead
10. Guiding with Grace: Raising Children with Compassion and Awareness
11. The Power of Positive Aging: Embracing Life After Fifty
12. Building Resilient Communities: Social Work in Action
13. The Ethical Educator: Principles for Teaching and Learning
14. From Insight to Impact: Social Psychology for a Better World
15. The Ethics of Empathy: A Guide to Ethical Living
16. The Science of Empowering the Self: Navigating Life's Challenges with Psychological Wisdom
17. The Mindful Conscious Leader: Meditation Techniques for Modern Management
18. Pioneering Spirit: Women's Pathways to Leadership and Empowerment
19. Feeling to Healing: The Role of Emotional Intelligence in Child Development
20. Transformative Talks and Words of Inspiration: Insights into Motivational Oratory

ৡৡৡ

Contact

Dr. Minakshi Bansal
Social Activist
Ahmedabad, Gujarat, Bharat
minakshiindiag20@yahoo.com

❧❧❧

|| LOKAHA SAMASTHAHA SUKHINO BHAVANTU ||